WORLD ORGANIZATIONS
International Red Cross

Ralf Perkins

W

FRANKLIN WATTS

A Division of Scholastic Inc.

NEW YORK TORONTO LONDON AUCKLAND SYDNEY
MEXICO CITY NEW DELHI HONG KONG
DANBURY, CONNECTICUT

First published in 2001 by Franklin Watts
96 Leonard Street, London EC2A 4XD

© Franklin Watts 2001

Editor: Rachel Cooke
Designer: Simon Borrough
Picture Research: Sue Mennell

This is a book about the International Red Cross
and Red Crescent Movement

Franklin Watts thanks the Red Cross Movement for
its cooperation and advice in producing this book,
but would like to make it clear that this is not a Red
Cross publication.

A CIP Catalog record for this title is available from
the Library of Congress Cataloging-in-Publication
Data.

ISBN   0-531-14623-5 (lib. bdg.)
        0-531-14812-2 (pbk.)

Printed in Malaysia

Picture credits:
Cover images: Topham Picturepoint/
Associated Press (left); Panos Pictures/Zed
Nelson (top right); British Red Cross
Society (bottom left)
Inside: AKG London pp. 4t, 4b; British
Red Cross Society pp. 1, 9, 11, 12l, 12r,
23t, 25, 27t; Corbis pp. 5 (Bill Gentile),
7t (Reuters New Media Inc.), 8t (Joseph
Sohm/ChromoSohm Inc), 24 (Liba
Taylor), 26 (Liba Taylor); International
Committee of the Red Cross pp. 15
(Thierry Gassmann), 19b (Boris Heger),
28t (Till Mayer); International Federation
of Red Cross and Red Crescent Societies
pp. 3, 7b, 10b, 27b (Lars Schwetije), 28b;
Magnum Photos p. 29b (David Hurn);
Popperfoto 13t, 14t; Popperfoto/Reuters pp.
1r (Rafiqur Rahman), 2t (Sergei Teterin), 2-3
(Yves Herman), 6 (Sergei Teterin), 8b (Mona
Sharaf), 10t (Yves Herman), 13b (Yuri Tutor), 14-
15, 16, 17l (Damir Sagoli), 17r (El Tiempo), 18, 19t
(Chor Sokunthea), 20l (Christian Charisius), 20r
(Rafiqur Rahman), 21 (Henry Romero) 22 (Michael
Dalder), 29t (Philippe Wojazer).

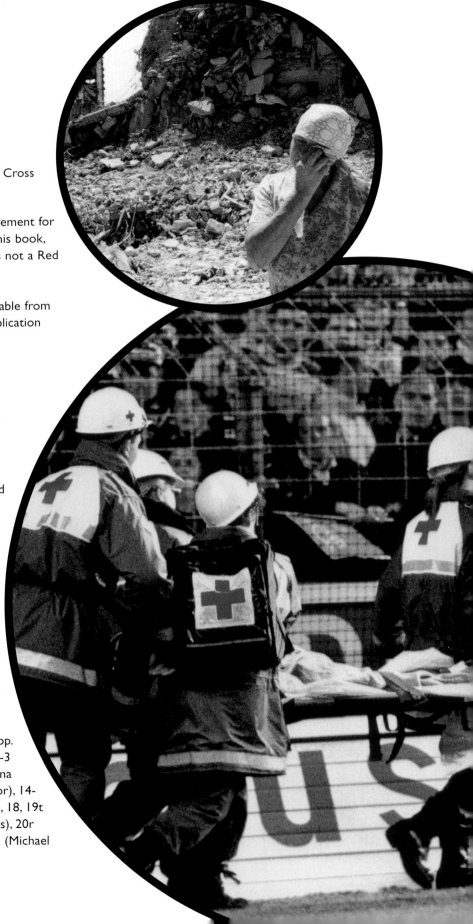

Contents

▲ *The emblems of the International Red Cross and Red Crescent Movement*

1. The Founding of the Red Cross

The Red Cross provides help for people in need or in a crisis — whether the crisis be caused by war, disaster, accidents, or more day-to-day problems such as poor health. The Movement (as it is often called) is one of the oldest and largest independent humanitarian organizations in the world.

◀ Henry Dunant, the Red Cross founder

▶ An early Red Cross volunteer helps the injured in war-torn Paris in 1870.

The Battle of Solferino

The Red Cross began in the mid-1800s, when one man told the world about the brutality of war.

On June 24, 1859, the French and Italian armies won a savage battle against the Austrians at Solferino in northern Italy. By nightfall, the armies had gone, but they left behind more than 40,000 dead and injured soldiers.

Henry Dunant, a young Swiss businessman, was shocked by the soldiers' terrible suffering. He gathered together a little group of local women and passing travelers to help. They cared for the wounded, comforted the dying, and buried the dead. The helpers came from different countries, but they all worked together. Later, Dunant said proudly that they had been *tutti fratelli* — "all brothers."

Problem

Whom Should You Help?

When faced with many injured people, whom do you help and whom do you treat first? At Solferino, Dunant helped wounded soldiers from both sides. He felt no one should be denied help who needed it, but that the people suffering the most should be treated first. This idea of impartiality has been a guiding principle of the Red Cross ever since. The Movement helps people because they need it, regardless of their nationality, race, religion, or political beliefs.

▼ A Red Cross worker waves the Red Cross flag during the civil war in El Salvador in 1989. The protective flag shows that he is neutral and not involved in the conflict.

Permanent National Relief Societies

In 1862, Dunant published A Memoir of Solferino, revealing the horrors of war. In it Dunant called for permanent relief societies in each country to train and equip volunteers to look after soldiers who were wounded in war. These volunteers would be attached to their country's armies and would assist any soldier who needed medical help or comfort.

Several Swiss gentlemen agreed with Dunant's humanitarian aims. At a meeting in Geneva on February 17, 1863, Dunant and four others formed the International Committee for Relief to the Wounded, which later became the International Committee of the Red Cross (ICRC).

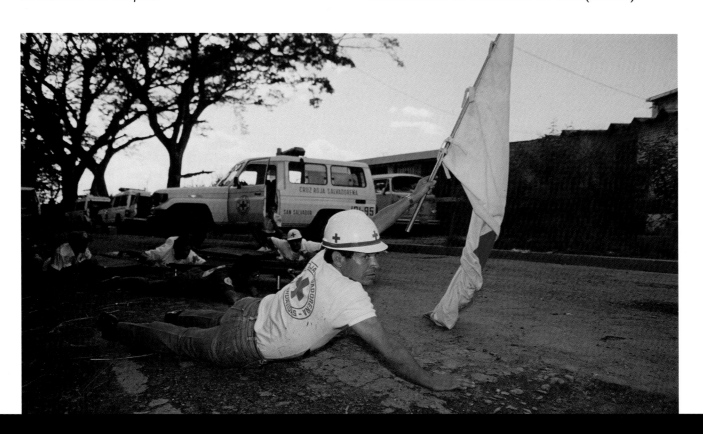

The Geneva Conventions

The Red Cross idea quickly won support from other European countries, such as Belgium, Denmark, and Portugal. At Geneva in 1864, delegates from twelve different countries framed a set of rules about how to treat wounded soldiers and medical workers in war. This was the original Geneva Convention.

No one before had tried to make general international laws about armed conflict or war, now called humanitarian law. The ICRC helped change all this. Since 1864, the Geneva Convention has been revised several times to cover different types of war victims. Today, there are four Geneva Conventions, and the governments of 189 countries have signed them. If they break these laws, government officials and army commanders can be prosecuted for war crimes.

Checklist

Humanitarian Laws

The four Geneva Conventions aim to protect wounded and sick members of the armed forces on land and at sea, prisoners of war, and civilians (people not members of the armed forces) in times of war. These are some of their rules:

- It is forbidden to kill or injure an enemy who surrenders.
- The wounded and sick shall be cared for by the people who have captured them.
- Prisoners of war and captured civilians shall be treated with respect. They shall be allowed to communicate with their families.
- It is forbidden to make a deliberate attack on civilians or their property.

▼ *This woman in Grozny, Chechnya, has lost her house in a Russian bombing raid. If this was a deliberate act, it would break one of the Geneva Conventions.*

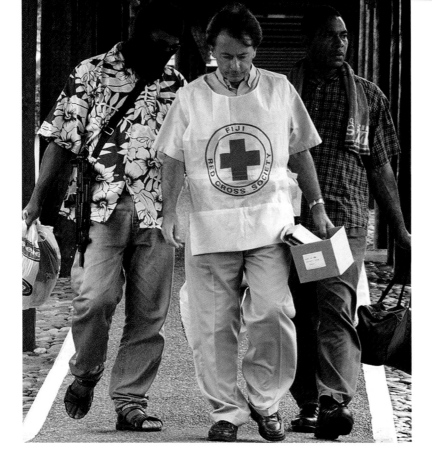

▲ *John Scott, director-general of the Fiji Red Cross, visits the hostages in the Fiji parliament in May 2000. The rebels holding the hostages were later arrested, and the ICRC now visits them.*

 # Spotlight

Being Neutral

The Red Cross Movement is neutral. It does not take sides in times of war or other conflict, nor does it involve itself in controversial debates, such as those surrounding politics or religion. In Fiji in 2000, armed rebels took 31 people (including the Fijian prime minister) hostage for 8 weeks and demanded a change in government. During the crisis, the director-general of the Fiji Red Cross, John Scott, visited the hostages every day, taking essential supplies and exchanging letters. The rebels only let him help the hostages because they knew that the Red Cross was neutral.

 # Spotlight

The Red Cross and Red Crescent Emblems

In 1863, the Red Cross's founding conference chose a red cross on a white background as the emblem for the volunteer medical personnel. This symbol (the reversed colors of the Swiss flag) may have been chosen as a tribute to Switzerland. However, the cross is also seen as a Christian symbol, and in fighting between Muslim Turks and Russian Christians in 1876, Turkish Red Cross workers wore a red crescent instead. Governments later recognized the symbol, and the two emblems are now used around the world as signs of neutral and impartial care; neither has any religious or national significance.

▲ *The Red Cross and Red Crescent flags fly alongside each other. They are special symbols protected by law.*

The Red Cross Grows

The drawing up of the first Geneva Convention attracted support around the world. Within 10 years, there were 22 National Red Cross Committees (later Societies) in Europe, including the British Red Cross in 1870 and the Danish in 1876. The American Red Cross was founded in 1881. There are now 176 recognized National Societies around the world.

All the National Societies were founded to provide assistance to the sick and wounded in times of war. However, it soon became apparent that there were other times when their skills could be useful — in times of disaster, such as floods or famine, or in training others to deal with emergency situations.

▶ An American Red Cross disaster truck, ready to carry aid to people hit by floods, fire, and storms

▼ A German Red Cross rescue worker searches for survivors in a collapsed building in Cairo in 1996.

Spotlight

Peacetime Disaster Relief

In September 1881, a forest fire raced across the state of Michigan, killing hundreds of people and leaving thousands homeless. Clara Barton, the founder of the American Red Cross, took building tools, clothes, and cash to help the fire's victims. In 1882–83, she helped flood victims in Mississippi, and in 1891, she sent food to starving peasants in Russia.

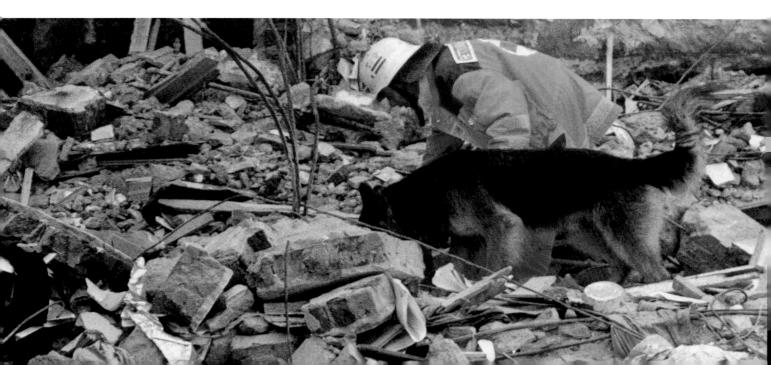

2. A Worldwide Movement

Today the Red Cross is a vast international Movement, with over 127 million members in 176 countries. Each part of this Movement is independent from the other, but all parts are united by shared goals and ideals.

The International Committee of the Red Cross

The International Committee of the Red Cross (ICRC) is the founding body of the organization. It is still based in Geneva, but it employs delegates from all around the world. The International Committee is particularly concerned with the protection of people during armed conflict, including civilians and prisoners of war, and it works with the National Societies to achieve its goal. The ICRC has been instrumental in the drawing up and amending of the Geneva Conventions, and it promotes humanitarian law.

▲ The headquarters of the ICRC in Geneva. Its French name is Comité International de la Croix-Rouge.

 Checklist

The different parts of the Red Cross and Red Crescent Movement are

- The International Committee of the Red Cross (ICRC)
- The International Federation of Red Cross and Red Crescent Societies
- 176 National Red Cross and National Red Crescent Societies

The National Societies

There are 176 recognized National Societies, such as the Japanese Red Cross and the Iranian Red Crescent. To qualify as a member of the Red Cross Movement, a Society must meet certain criteria. For example, each Society must be legally recognized by its country as an independent voluntary aid organization that provides support to the country's public authorities. This enables the Societies to support their country's army medical services in wartime, and the civilian medical and emergency services at all times. It also means that a Society can give care to anyone who needs it, regardless of nationality.

▲ Red Cross volunteers assist a spectator who was injured when a stand collapsed at a soccer match in Brussels.

A Range of Services

In addition to its emergency role, each National Society provides a range of support services, which vary from country to country. For example, the American Red Cross provides a blood donation service, but the British Red Cross does not. Many Societies provide first-aid stations at sporting events, rock concerts, and festivals. Often they teach first aid to schools, clubs, and businesses. They also provide funding and expertise for the international Movement.

The International Federation

The National Societies all belong to one big group called the International Federation of Red Cross and Red Crescent Societies. The International Federation coordinates disaster relief provided by the different Societies and helps the National Societies develop their services. In addition, it assists countries that want to set up Societies.

 Spotlight

International Support

After a massive earthquake in Turkey left more than 300,000 people homeless in 1999, the International Federation of Red Cross and Red Crescent Societies immediately sent an assessment team to meet with the Turkish authorities to find out how they could help. At the same time, the National Societies launched appeals to raise funds for this assistance. The British Red Cross provided a logistics expert for the assessment team and raised nearly $3 million in its appeal.

▼ After an earthquake in Turkey in 1999, the International Federation worked with the Turkish Red Crescent to provide relief.

Working Together

Representatives from the National Societies, the International Federation, and the International Committee regularly meet with the governments of countries that have signed the Geneva Conventions to discuss the principles that unite the Movement and other matters of common humanitarian concern. These conferences usually take place once every four years. At a conference in 1965, the Red Cross and Red Crescent Movement agreed to seven Fundamental Principles, which are based on the ideas that formed the Movement and are upheld today.

▲ Delegates from the International Red Cross and Red Crescent Movement meet in Birmingham, England, in 1993.

✓ Checklist

The Fundamental Principles of the Red Cross

Humanity: The Movement aims to prevent and lessen human suffering wherever it may be found.

Impartiality — see page 5.

Neutrality — see page 7.

Independence — the National Societies, while supporting their governments, remain independent.

Voluntary Service — see page 12.

Unity — there can be only one Red Cross or Red Crescent Society in any one country. It must be open to all.

Universality — the Movement is a worldwide one, where all the Societies share equal status and responsibilities.

Who Pays for the Red Cross?

The Red Cross needs a large amount of money to carry out its work around the world. In 2000, the International Committee in Geneva spent approximately one billion Swiss francs (about $550 million). This does not include the money spent by National Societies.

All of this money is donated, some of it through the National Societies. A lot of it comes from governments and international bodies such as the European Union. The Red Cross does not accept donations that would require it to act against its Fundamental Principles. For example, a government that gives money to help refugees cannot demand that the money assist people of only one nationality or race.

Private Donations

Private individuals and companies also give money to the Red Cross. Private donations are vital when a disaster strikes. If Armenia suffers an earthquake or Ethiopia faces famine, the Red Cross asks people all over the world for donations to help the victims of that disaster. It runs appeals on television and in newspapers.

Spotlight

World Red Cross and Red Crescent Day

Every year May 8, Henry Dunant's birthday, is celebrated as World Red Cross and Red Crescent Day. On this day the Red Cross makes a worldwide appeal for donations, and it encourages newspapers and television stations to publicize its work. Red Cross volunteers collect money from the public, and people wear Red Cross badges.

A Voluntary Workforce

People who work for the Red Cross do so because they want to help others of their own free will, not because they expect to make money from it. This voluntary service is an important principle of the Red Cross. In the vast majority of cases, it means that the volunteers give their time for free.

However, all sections of the Red Cross have paid employees, too. Delegates work for the international sections of the Movement, although some are supported financially by the National Societies. These delegates are skilled workers, such as health coordinators and engineers, who can be sent to any part of the world to relieve human suffering in wars and disasters.

▲ *Sales of seasonal cards raise money for some National Societies.*

▲ *A Red Cross helper asks for donations from the public.*

Warfare has changed since Henry Dunant's lifetime. Weapons are deadlier, and civilians often suffer in war as much as soldiers do. Through two world wars and many subsequent conflicts, the Red Cross has adapted to these changes as it continues to provide neutral support to those in need.

✓ Checklist

During the Gulf War in 1990, American Red Cross workers provided humanitarian assistance to the U.S. Armed Forces by

- carrying 215,000 messages to and from the troops.
- providing comfort and support to the injured and soldiers in need.
- supporting 4,700 military families back home with $1.72 million in financial assistance and other services.

▲ Australian Red Cross workers staff an emergency medical post for wounded soldiers in New Guinea during World War II (1939–45).

Battlefield Support

The Red Cross's original war work remains vital. In World War I (1914–18), Red Cross Societies provided nurses and other staff to treat the injured. Today, when most armies provide their own medical services, the National Societies often support their armies in different ways — helping soldiers remain in contact with their families at home or visiting injured troops in the hospital.

▲ Russian women ask an ICRC worker to help them trace their husbands and sons who are fighting in the Russian conflict in Chechnya in 1995.

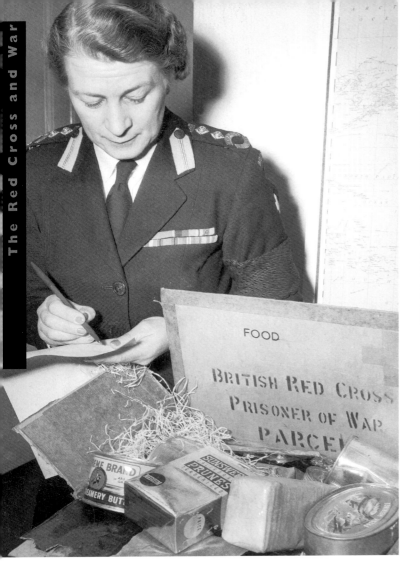

▲ A British Red Cross worker checks care parcels to be sent to prisoners of war in Korea in 1952.

Since the 1970s, an armed group called the Polisario Front has held nearly two thousand Moroccans captive in the western Sahara Desert. Every year ICRC delegates visit these forgotten prisoners, taking them news and family letters and providing medical assistance. In February 2000, 126 elderly and ill prisoners were released. The Polisario Front and the Moroccan government used the ICRC as a neutral go-between in the release process.

Prisoners of War

In most conflicts, soldiers and civilians are taken prisoner on both sides. The Third Geneva Convention recognizes the role of the ICRC as a neutral organization whose representatives must be allowed to visit these prisoners. ICRC delegates visit prisoners of war and try to put them in touch with their families. They make sure that prisoners have proper food and medical care and that they are not being mistreated.

▲ *The Red Cross Movement provides food for civilians forced to flee their homes during war.*

▼ *Red Cross nurses give emergency aid to man wounded in Rwanda's civil war in April 1995.*

Protecting Civilians

A major part of the Red Cross's wartime work today is helping civilians. When fighting breaks out, the ICRC, working with the National Societies, tries to maintain basic medical supplies, food, and water services, so that ordinary people do not die of starvation or disease while the fighting rages around them. It sets up refugee shelters for people who are forced out of their homes. It also collects names and photographs of missing people and tries to trace them in enemy prisons, refugee camps, or among the dead.

If necessary, the ICRC supplies trained medical teams to assist in local hospitals that cannot cope with the demand on their resources. ICRC surgeons train local doctors to deal with wounds that are inflicted in a war, so that they can take over once the ICRC team has moved on.

When the Fighting Stops

War leaves behind many people who suffer long after the fighting has stopped. Some victims of war have physical problems, such as injuries caused by a bomb. Some have emotional problems as well. Red Cross workers help all these people. They organize the rebuilding of hospitals and schools. They provide seeds, fertilizer, and equipment so farming can begin again. Counselors help people understand the horrible things they have seen in war. Researchers reunite missing people with their families.

▼ *Young refugees from Rwanda in an ICRC truck. They have been separated from their families by civil war.*

Spotlight

Reuniting Families

When fighting in the Korean War stopped in 1953, many families were divided between North and South Korea. In 2000, the two Korean governments agreed that the two National Red Cross Societies could organize some family reunions. Park Yoon-sung, age 85, lives in South Korea. The Red Cross escorted him to North Korea to meet his two brothers. "I never dreamed of this happening," Park Yoon-sung said. "I miss my brothers so much."

The Horrors of War

At times of war, people and governments can do terrible things. People's human rights and humanitarian laws are often ignored. Some aid organizations speak out publicly against human rights abuses they witness, but the Red Cross rarely publicly criticizes or condemns any government. The Red Cross in no way ignores violations of human rights or humanitarian law, but it expresses its concerns privately. Otherwise, a government might stop seeing the Red Cross as neutral and may stop its workers from helping the people who are suffering.

Problem

Aid for Serbia

In the early 1990s, Serbia was at the center of a series of conflicts in the former Yugoslavia, fighting in Croatia, Bosnia, and Kosovo. The Serbian government was severely criticized for its conduct in these wars. Despite this, the ICRC continued to support the Yugoslav (Serbian) Red Cross in its humanitarian aid for Serb civilians and refugees. Some other aid agencies refused to help because of Serbia's human rights record.

▲ Kosovan refugees, forced from their homes by Serbs in 1999, are helped by the Red Cross Movement.

Awareness of the Limits on War

The Red Cross Movement constantly promotes humanitarian principles and rules through its support of the Geneva Conventions. Both the ICRC and National Societies publish books and leaflets on the Conventions. Red Cross delegates teach humanitarian law to the armed forces, to the general public, and to children. In a civil war, the ICRC tries to ensure that all sides in the conflict are informed of humanitarian law and how it affects them.

▲ Red Cross workers are caught in the middle of fighting between government and rebel troops in Colombia, 2000.

Spotlight

Learning the Law

Some National Red Cross Societies, including Russia and Belgium, organize "trial trials." Groups of law students come together to practice war crimes trials, with actors playing the accused and experts on hand to give advice. In this way, students learn about humanitarian law and the problems lawyers face when trying to prove a person is guilty of breaking the law or defending such a person.

New Technology

In promoting the Geneva Conventions, the ICRC reminds people that they have a responsibility in choosing what weapons they use. Today, advances in technology mean that ever more terrifying weapons can be invented. In 1998, Dr. Cornelio Sommaruga, president of the ICRC, warned against these developments: "International humanitarian law has an essential role to play in sparing humanity the worst consequences of its technical capabilities."

Checklist

International humanitarian laws ban the use of certain weapons as inhumane. These include

- bullets that shatter when they hit a person
- chemical weapons — bombs that release poison gas
- biological weapons — bombs that release the germs of a deadly disease
- antipersonnel land mines — devices, buried underground, that explode when someone steps on them
- laser weapons that are designed to cause permanent blindness

Problem

Antipersonnel Land Mines

Although there is a treaty banning these mines, some countries have not yet signed it, and many armies still use them. Buried underground, mines stay active for years after a war is over. Every hour, somewhere in the world, three people are killed or maimed by a mine.

▼ An Iranian child lies in a hospital, a victim of a chemical attack made by Iraq during the Iran-Iraq war in 1988. The chemicals have burned his skin and caused severe blistering.

⬤ Spotlight

The ICRC has set up more than thirty workshops around the world to produce the artificial limbs, crutches, and wheelchairs that the victims of land mines need. They try to use cheap, easily available materials and train local staff, so that the workshops can eventually operate independently.

◀ *Soccer star David Ginola visits an artificial limb workshop in Cambodia, where many people have been maimed by antipersonnel land mines.*

◖ Problem

New Weapons

After the war in Kosovo in 1999, people were at risk not only from mines planted by the Serbian forces but also from some unexploded cluster bombs dropped by the NATO forces. NATO was fighting to protect the Kosovar Albanians from the Serbs. Cluster bombs are not banned because they are designed to explode on impact, but a small percentage do not.

A cluster bomb looks like a soda can with a parachute attached, and could be mistaken for a toy. Some Kosovar children have been killed by them. The ICRC trained six people in mine awareness to teach Kosovars about the dangers of mines. They included cluster bombs in their lessons.

▲ *Children in Kosovo read leaflets handed out by the ICRC warning them about the dangers of mines and unexploded bombs left over from the war in 1999.*

4. When Disaster Strikes

The **Red Cross Movement** has been helping victims of peacetime disasters for almost 120 years. The National Societies provide assistance first, but when a major disaster occurs, the International Federation of Red Cross and Red Crescent Societies coordinates help from around the world.

▲ *The German Red Cross sends trucks fully loaded with supplies to hurricane-hit Honduras in 1998.*

▶ *Flooding is a major problem for Bangladesh. This is its capital, Dhaka, in 1998.*

Natural Disasters

Natural disasters are often caused by unusual weather or sudden changes in the Earth's surface. Heavy rains might cause flooding or landslides. An earthquake at sea might push a huge tidal wave over coastal villages.

The International Federation provides help wherever the need is greatest. This means many of its resources are directed toward poorer, developing countries that are less prepared for emergencies.

The World Disasters Report

After each disaster is over, the Red Cross Movement studies its relief work and considers how to improve it next time. Each year, the International Federation publishes the World Disasters Report. This shows which countries are likely to suffer most from disasters. It advises how to improve warning systems and emergency services. It helps the Red Cross and others plan for future disasters.

Emergency Relief

In any disaster, the Red Cross's first duty is to help where the need is greatest. It works alongside the emergency services as they rescue people caught in the disaster and treat severely injured people. The National Societies provide first-aid assistance and distribute emergency supplies.

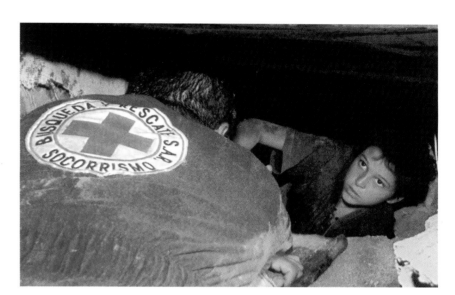

A Red Cross worker helps ▲ rescue a boy trapped in ruins after an earthquake in Colombia in 1999.

Polluted water causes epidemics of cholera and diarrhea, and these diseases often kill more people than the disaster itself. The Red Cross brings in supplies of clean drinking water for disaster victims or provides water-purifying tablets. It helps ensure that safe, permanent water supplies are restored as soon as possible.

 Spotlight

Working with Others

The National Societies and the International Federation of Red Cross and Red Crescent Societies do not just work with each other and the authorities in a disaster-stricken country. They also work with other aid agencies, such as the World Health Organization, which can provide different expertise.

As much as possible, during and after an emergency, the Red Cross tries to work with the local businesses and laborers. This supports the local economy and contributes to the long-term recovery of the area.

▲ A temporary Red Crescent tent city put up in Turkey for people made homeless by the earthquake in 1999

Food and Shelter

The Red Cross also arranges food and shelter for people who have been made homeless. It sets up hostels in big buildings such as churches and town halls or erects temporary "tent cities." When a crisis is over, Red Cross workers help people return home. If needed, they hand out tools and building materials for people to repair or rebuild their houses. In rural areas they provide seeds and agricultural equipment to allow people to plant new crops.

 Problem

Coordinating Disaster Relief

In the floods in Mozambique in February 2000, more than 540,000 people lost their homes. Aid poured in: governments sent helicopters and planes, and thousands of aid agencies sent teams to help. "It was like a circus," commented one senior aid worker. The Mozambique government initially struggled to coordinate the relief. Some tasks were done twice, and help was given where it wasn't needed. Advised by the Mozambique Red Cross Society, the government set up daily briefings for both the press and aid agencies and ensured that aid agencies acted with their knowledge and consent.

▶ The Mozambique Red Cross sends out boats to distribute aid and rescue people trapped by flood waters in March 2000.

Preparing for the Worst

The Red Cross works to lessen the impact of disasters. It provides warning and rescue systems that communities can organize by themselves. During the Mozambique floods in 2000, other countries sent helicopters to pluck people to safety from trees and rooftops. Mozambique cannot afford a permanent rescue system based on helicopters, however. It is simpler and cheaper to provide small boats to be stored in areas at risk of flooding, so that when floods happen, local people can rescue each other.

▶ A Red Crescent volunteer helps a young child who has lost her home in floods in Bangladesh in 1998.

 Spotlight

Flood Alert

In 1991, flooding in Bangladesh killed 140,000 people. In 1998, the floods were worse, but fewer than 1,000 people died. Many lives were saved in 1998 because the International Federation had helped set up a storm warning system. When a storm or cyclone is coming, thousands of volunteers from the Bangladeshi Red Crescent travel up and down the coast using megaphones to tell people to shift to higher ground. The Red Cross Movement also helped build cyclone shelters and artificial hills where people can take shelter until a storm is over.

Problem

The Poverty Trap
Many disasters are caused by humans, and they could be avoided. In July 2000, over 150 people living at a garbage dump in Manila died when a towering mountain of trash collapsed in heavy rains, smothering their shanty huts. The victims were some of the poorest people in the Philippines: garbage pickers who sift through dumps looking for items to sell on the streets. The Red Cross always helps in disasters like these, but it also works to provide better living conditions for people.

◀ *The Gambian Red Cross gives lessons in AIDS awareness to a group of villagers.*

Silent Disasters
People give generously to Red Cross appeals for victims of earthquakes, floods, and hurricanes. These are big, dramatic disasters that everyone sees on television. But the Red Cross needs money for "silent disasters" too. These are long-term problems, such as poverty and disease, to which people do not give as much money.

In parts of Africa, AIDS is a "silent disaster." AIDS is gradually killing millions of people. It destroys families and damages national economies. The Red Cross trains local workers to give advice about AIDS. It funds hospitals to care for the sick and runs orphanages and schools to protect children whose parents have died.

 # Spotlight

Teaching Your Friends
The International Federation encourages the National Societies to train young volunteers in AIDS education. Young people listen to people of their own age more willingly than older authority figures. The Federation supports the Societies by publishing a training manual for young people called *Action with Youth*.

24

5. Caring for the Community

Many people know the Red Cross through the work of the National Societies in their local communities. They provide long- and short-term support to those in need.

▼ *Some National Societies offer transportation to people who cannot travel by themselves.*

 Checklist

Various Red Cross National Societies provide the following community services:

- The short-term loan of medical equipment such as wheelchairs
- Transportation or escorts for elderly and ill people so they can make essential trips
- Care for people who have just come out of the hospital or whose regular caretakers are away
- Helping people trace and contact their families overseas who are separated from them by war
- First-aid training and support at public events

First Aid

Accidents can happen to anyone anywhere — in the home, at work, in a car. First aid is the immediate medical care that is given to accident victims before a doctor or ambulance arrives. It includes stopping heavy bleeding, resuscitating someone who has stopped breathing, and cooling burns. Prompt first aid can mean the difference between an accident victim living or dying.

RELIEF ORGANIZATIONS (OTHER THAN RED CROSS)

FIRST-AID KIT

▲ The red cross symbol is often misused. A white cross on green is a recognized symbol for first-aid.

Problem

A Sign of Protection

The red cross symbol is so often associated with first aid and medical care that people who are not involved in military medical services or the Movement sometimes use it too. This is against the law in nearly all countries. The Geneva Conventions recognize the symbol as a special one that protects the wounded and sick, and those who have official permission to help them, in times of war. It is important that its effect not be weakened by unauthorized use. The Red Cross Societies work with their governments to stop illegal uses of the cross or crescent symbol.

National Red Cross and Red Crescent Societies' volunteers provide first aid service at big public events to deal with emergencies. They also teach first aid to anyone who wishes to learn it, including children as young as five. The Red Cross sells first-aid courses and first-aid kits to businesses, schools, and sports clubs. The money raised from these sales funds other Red Cross work. Some Societies teach first aid to children for free.

◄ A woman learns how to bandage a wound at a first-aid class run by the Red Cross in the Gambia.

Blood Banks

In many countries, the National Red Cross or Red Crescent Society runs a blood donation service, or "blood bank." The Red Cross encourages healthy citizens to give some of their blood to help others. The blood is labeled and stored by hospitals to be used when someone needs extra blood during surgery, or to replace blood a person has lost in a car crash or other accident.

▲ A blood donation service run by the Cambodian Red Cross

A Friend in Need

The Red Cross and Red Crescent Societies around the world are active in many areas where people need help. Some provide clothing and emergency supplies for families whose houses have burned down, for example.

Home visits can be a lifeline for an elderly or ill person. Some Societies provide nurses to make regular visits. Others help when someone who cares for an ill or elderly relative has to go into the hospital. The volunteer looks after the relative in his or her absence. Red Cross volunteers also drive patients to and from the hospital if they are not well enough to make the trip by themselves.

 Spotlight

Medical Research

The Red Cross's medical work, both at war and in peacetime, has led some Societies to be involved in medical research. In 1998, the American Red Cross and the U.S. Army invented a bandage that contains a special blood-clotting agent that stops bleeding quickly. This research is useful not just for work in war zones. The same bandages will save lives in peacetime emergencies, such as car accidents and earthquakes.

◀ A Red Cross volunteer in Bosnia helps an elderly man in his home.

Problem

Care in War

The Sierra Leone Red Cross Society runs health clinics, blood banks, and projects within local communities to improve knowledge of health care and risks. In 1999, a civil war began in the country. The Society tried to maintain its everyday care, along with helping with the wounded and displaced people. Some of its branch offices were looted, and worse still, some of its volunteers were killed. As soon as peace returned to its country, the Society began to rebuild its community services.

▲ In Sierra Leone, where civil war has damaged normal health services, the ICRC helps run hospitals for civilians.

▲ In Belarus, a doctor supported by the International Federation of Red Cross and Red Crescent Societies checks a boy for thyroid deficiency.

Helping Others

The Red Cross's care and support services improve life for people who are sick, elderly, or simply alone. The National Societies can only help because of their volunteers — people who give up some of their time to help others in need. The principles that guide the Movement in times of war and disaster are just as important at a community level.

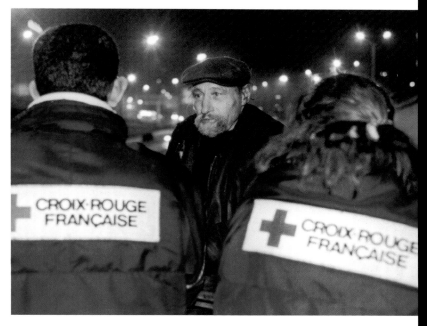

▲ *Two volunteers from the French Red Cross offer help to a homeless man living under a bridge in Paris.*

▼ *Young volunteers learn babysitting skills in Arizona. American Red Cross workers teach the students how to protect babies from accidents and injuries.*

Spotlight

The Year of the Volunteer

On December 5, 2000, the United Nations launched its International Year of the Volunteer to recognize and promote the work of volunteers around the world. Speaking at the opening ceremony, Dr. Astrid Heidberg, president of the International Federation of Red Cross and Red Crescent Societies, said: "Everyone likes to make a difference in life... Today we are launching a year to celebrate and promote the hundreds of millions of unselfish women and men, young and old, who give their time and energy to make a difference to the lives of others."

 ## Checklist

Red Cross Youth

Anyone can become a Red Cross or Red Crescent volunteer. Societies around the world particularly encourage young people to get involved. Here are just some of the activities of the Red Cross Youth in Denmark:

- holiday camps
- campaigns against racism
- rock concerts
- tree planting in Africa
- playgrounds for children in asylum centers
- first-aid courses for young people

aid — help or assistance; the organized help given to suffering people or poor countries by groups such as the Red Cross and UNICEF

AIDS — **A**cquired **I**mmune **D**eficiency **S**yndrome; a disease that weakens and kills people by destroying their body's ability to fight off common illnesses

asylum — a place of safety and protection

civil war — a war fought between people living in the same country or of the same nationality

convention — an agreement or contract signed by different countries on an important issue

criteria — standards; conditions or rules that someone has to accept if he or she wishes to join a particular group or society

cyclone — a tornado; a storm with strong circular winds and heavy rains

diarrhea — a stomach illness that drains the water from a person's body; it can kill babies and young children

humanitarian — concerned with the happiness, safety, and welfare of people

impartiality — treating everyone in the same way regardless of their race, nationality, or religion

logistics — organizational work, such as transportation and communication, that makes sure help reaches the people who need it

neutrality — not taking sides in any kind of debate or conflict

shanty huts — unsafe, poor housing made out of flimsy materials such as cardboard, bags, or sheets of tin

torture — deliberately causing intense pain to a person, as a punish-ment or to make him or her reveal a secret

vital — of the greatest importance; essential

war crime — a crime committed in war time that goes against the accepted codes of conduct in war, such as the Geneva Conventions

Useful Information

International Committee of the Red Cross
Public Information Centre
19 Avenue de la Paix
CH 1202 Genève
Switzerland
www.icrc.org

**International Federation of Red Cross
and Red Crescent Societies**
P.O. Box 372
CH 1211 Geneva 19
Switzerland
www.ifrc.org

**To find postal addresses and Web sites for
the National Societies:**
www.ifrc.org/address

Some National Society addresses:

American Red Cross
431 18th Street N.W., 2nd Floor
Washington, DC 20006
www.redcross.org

British Red Cross
9 Grosvenor Crescent
London SW1X 7EJ
UK
www.redcross.org.uk

Australian Red Cross
P.O. Box 196
Carlton South, VIC, 3053
Australia
www.redcross.org.au

Canadian Red Cross Society
170 Metcalfe Street, Suite 300
Ottawa
Ontario K2P 2P2
Canada
www.redcross.ca

Danish Red Cross
P.O. Box 2600
DK–2100 Köbenhavn Ö
Denmark
www.redcross.dk

New Zealand Red Cross
P.O. Box 12–140
Thorndon
Wellington 6038
New Zealand
www.redcross.org.nz

**For information on other humanitarian
relief work:**
www.reliefweb.int

**United Nations Office for the
Coordination of Humanitarian Affairs**
www.reliefweb.int/ocha_ol/index.html

World Health Organization
www.who.int

Index